GIVE UP TO GAIN

*A revolutionary, new, old way to find more time to do whatever
you want to do.*

Also by J Edward Frank

Fortysomething Dad Self Help Stories
Give up to Gain

Watch for more at https://jedwardfrank.wordpress.com.

Table of Contents

To Fortysomething mom, Eightsomething son, and Fiveorsixsomething daughter for all their help even when they don't know about it.

Prologue

"If you want to try something new in life, you've got to give up something else that's already wasting time." a best-selling, unknown Japanese author.

Grave Digger

A silent shadow snuck noisily out through the cemetery ignoring all writing conventions and using as many lovely adverbs as he wanted. The leaves crackled underfoot and the twigs snapped as he tried not to make a sound.

"Why are there leaves and sticks in a cemetery with no trees?" the not-so-silent, not-so-young man whispered just below a grunt. He hefted his load up a little higher on his shoulder. The bag looked almost empty.

Forty-something dad hurried through the graveside with all the tiny little graves and itty-bitty marking stones. This was his least favorite part. If only someone had come up with a better way of disposing of, well, you know.

"Late-night burial?" A creepy-looking man, who hadn't been there before, asked.

"You don't have a lot of teeth," Forty-something dad commented before he thought about what he was saying.

"You don't have a lot of manners," the creepy-looking man with not a lot of teeth said.

"Oh, I was just mentioning it because you have a toothpick in your mouth but you don't have teeth to pick."

"Can't be picky these days."

"Was that meant to be a really bad pun? Never mind. I've got to be going."

"Not until you finish what you came here for," Creepy said.

"I can do that some other time," Forty-something dad said.

"No no, that's what I'm here for."

"You are OK with what I am going to do?"

"No, I'm here to creep you out."

"Oh, good job."

"Hah hah, I'm here to help you out. You see what I did with that? One word will set your mind at ease and one will make you wet your pants."

"Yeah, I didn't like what you did with that."

"Still here to help you out. Do you want to use my shovel?"

Forty-something dad looked at The creepy man's large shovel. He bought the bag off his shoulder and held it up looking at a tiny little lump in the bottom.

"Um, that's a little big."

"What this?" Creepy man held up the shovel and started laughing again. "Oh no, that's my weapon," he chuckled and made a motion with the shovel as if he were smacking someone on the head. He pulled a small metal spoon out of his pocket and handed it over.

"Oh, thanks."

The middle age man accepted the non-mechanical, non-electronic antiquated utensil from the creepy man. He stared at it for a moment, disappointed thinking about how far technology has advanced in recent years but everyone was still eating and digging graves with a small piece of metal.

Forty-something dad set his bag and got to work. Fortunately, after a couple of scoops, he had a hole big enough for his cargo. He dropped a bag in and started to bury it.

"You might want to make it a little bit deeper," Creepy said a little creepier than usual.

"Why?" Forty-something dad swallowed hard.

"You never know when you might have regrets."

Forty-something dad was already having regrets about having come to this creepy cemetery. Couldn't he have just buried it in the backyard? No, what if he had, regrets. Oh no, the creepy guy was right. He pulled everything back out and dug the hole quite a bit deeper with a spoon.

By the time he had finished burying it much deeper, the creepy guy was gone. That was a good thing, or was it? Now in his place were a couple of other middle-aged men carrying almost empty bags and trying to sneak through the cemetery. Forty-something dad didn't try to hide it anymore. He'd done what he came here to do. He walked proudly out of the cemetery.

Forty-something mom was waiting for him when he got back. Sitting at the table drinking a cup of tea to calm her nerves.

"Did you do it?"

"Yeah," he walked over to the sink and started washing his hands. As he patted them dry on the towel he instinctively reached into his pocket and let out a little girly scream.

"My phone. I can't find my phone. I think I might've dropped it in the cemetery. I'll be back in five minutes."

He ran screaming back out the door. Forty-something mom calmly looked at the clock and waited. Thirty minutes later the door opened and Forty-something dad stumbled back in. He didn't bother to wash his hands this time.

"It's OK, I found it. I accidentally buried it in the cemetery."

"Accidentally? I thought that's what you went there to bury," Forty-something mom reminded him.

"Oh yeah, I guess I just can't give it up."

"You're calling me."

"Am I?" he pressed the end call button and quickly raised the phone to his ear.

"I am right next to you. You don't have to talk to me on the phone."

"Oh, that's OK."

"Now you're texting me."

"I guess I just can't give it up. I mean, I need it for work."

"That is a true excuse. Maybe you need to reevaluate your reasons for trying to give it up."

"Yeah, Why was I trying to give up the cell phone? Social reasons? Empathy? It's hard to be empathetic on the phone. Maybe it was for mental peace of mind? Meditation? I can't do meditation without my phone or was it the other way around? Spiritual? Supernatural? Are those the same thing?"

"I thought you said it was getting in the way. You had something you wanted to get done but you were spending too much time on your phone."

"Oh yeah, I want to write a book."

"What's the book about?"

"Oh, how you can get your goals accomplished if you give something up. Either that or a middle-grade fantasy adventure. You know, they are both so similar."

"OK, so, maybe you don't have to give something up completely? Maybe you just need to give up something at a certain time or a certain activity on a certain thing?"

"You're going somewhere with this. I like where you're going. Where are you going with this?"

"I think I'm already there."

"So, you're saying that I don't need to give up my phone completely. I just need to give up shopping for worthless stuff that I don't need for thirty minutes before bed?" Forty-something dad asked.

"Well, that's not exactly what I'm saying but if you read between the lines, that's exactly what I'm saying."

"But, what if I miss a good deal on an old retro video game system that I probably won't have time to use?" Forty-something dad intentionally dropped his jaw and forced air to rush into his mouth sounding much like Nintendo's Kirby or a Kirby vacuum cleaner.

"Does anybody really need that?"

"It's all about priorities."

"That word is not supposed to be pluralized."

"I get it. If I want to write a book more than I want to browse for shopping for something that I don't want to buy, I need to give up browsing for something I don't want to buy. I don't have to give up my phone."

"That is exactly what I said."

"I can't believe no one's ever thought of this before."

"I think a lot of people have thought of this before."

"Wait, how did people give up browsing on their smartphones to write a book before they ever were smartphones?"

Research

Forty-something dad held onto the curved lines of a giant letter S. It wasn't much, not the lifeboat he'd been hoping for. There just were no books about it. Well, no books in English.

He found a couple of articles about people giving up TV for a month or even a year. One girl wrote a book. That wasn't entirely not what he was looking for. He had wanted to write a book. The problem is, he never really watched much TV after the kids came along. Too much violence in anime. The kids could handle it better than he could.

Now he was lost in a sea of words trying to stay afloat. The internet was a good source of words but that's all it was. He couldn't even verify any of those words were true. Forty-something dad stuck his head back down below the surface of the words and peeked around again. If only he still had his secret x-ray goggles that could find information on demand.

"Ahoy there matey," someone called to him from across the sea of words.

"Pirates don't have Indian accents."

"I'm Canadian."

"Oh, sorry. I did some acting in college. Are you researching on how to get something done if you give up something?"

"No, I'm reading about the mating habits of independently own self-driving electric elephants."

"Why would you research that? And are you sure that's not a Russian accent?"

"I told you I'm from Kazakhstan and I'm not researching. You can't *research* on the internet. Even if you've looked it up before, it's still just *searching*. Right now I'm just following the white rabbit on a wild goose chase of articles that have nothing to do with the real reason I got on the search engine."

"Do I want to know?"

"Pre-emergent herbicides."

"Hold on, I actually think I've been down that rabbit hole. Then again, maybe every search query ends up with electric elephants.

"If you want my advice, and I do have a Ph.D. in advice-giving,"

"Psychology?" Forty-something dad interrupted. He had considered that as a career path but opted for a different doctorate only because it was also a doctorate degree.

"No, advice-giving. My advisor got tired of me giving her advice and told me I should get a degree in giving advice. So I made up my own doctorate. Now when people say 'why should I take advice from you?' I can give them a good reason."

"What kind of work do you do?

"I have a blog where I give advice on everything. Look, if you want my advice you should stop looking on the internet. Maybe you should give up the internet altogether. It's a good way to find out how to stop your toilet from ghost flushing but even those tips don't work. If you want to grow mentally and cognitively, stop looking at random articles on the internet. Stop shopping on the preowned thrift shop websites."

"And why should I take advice from you?"

"I thought I gave you the answer to that one already. Take some memory courses."

"No, I remember what you said. It's just that you are browsing random articles and it looks like that is a preowned shopping website on another tab on your phone," Forty-something dad reminded him.

"Didn't your dad ever tell you to do as I say, not as I do? I know what to do I just don't want to do it. If I could give up on browsing random articles and shopping for preowned stuff I'd have at least one more hour a day and probably another day every hour. I could do something productive that I really want to do. I've always wanted to write a book. I've always wanted to record an audiobook. Someday I'd even like to read a book."

"Books, it's just another big sea of words that I'll drown in. I'm stuck in a sea of words right now."

"Not books. Well, maybe now with self-publishing but the truth is, if someone goes through all the trouble of editing, hiring a cover artist, finding beta readers, editing again, hiring an editor, and marketing a book, there's at least a little more research that went into what they write."

"But I haven't been able to find any books about 'giving up something time and soul-consuming, to gain time and pursue true goals.'"

"That is a very specific search query. Broaden your search. Although, I'm not sure you need a book about that. Just that term right there should be enough for you. Just give something up, experiment. See how much time you gain. Find out for yourself how you will pursue your goals and your passion. If you do end up writing a book about it, make sure you use that exact search term for your keywords or no one will want to read it."

"Wow, that's the lifeboat I've been looking for in the sea of words."

"The word lifeboat floated just past the two of them. Forty-something dad let go of his S and swam across to the lifeboat. He climbed on board and reached out for the other stranger.

"No, I think I'll research electric elephants a little bit more so I can give advice on them. You go give something up so that you can pursue your true passions and good luck to you."

"Good luck to you as well."

"I don't need luck. I'm browsing the internet and reading stupid articles. I need psychological counseling."

He surfed the lifeboat back to shore where Forty-something mom helped him off and back onto the back deck.

"I just read this great book about a guy who is successful because he gave up some worthless time-consuming habits and pursued his passion. I wish I could translate it for you. It's in Japanese."

"You don't have to. I think what you just told me was everything I've been looking for."

Clarity

"**I** thought you were going to write a book?" Forty-something mom asked.

"I am. I'll start later," Forty-something dad answered.

"You did say that was your priority. That was what you wanted to do and why you were going to give up wasting time on your phone or the internet.

"Yup, don't worry. I'm not wasting time right now, I'm procrastinating."

"Isn't that the same thing?"

Forty-something dad's eyes grew wide as he tried to pull them narrow. He quickly stuck his phone under his leg and crossed his hands in his lap.

"I saw you put your phone under your leg. I'm not trying to hold you accountable. I was just asking."

Only then did he realize that he was supposed to be hiding the phone from himself. Instead of hiding his procrastination, he needed to hide the phone so he didn't use it to procrastinate.

"But, it's so easy to start procrastinating with my phone. It's just right here. I mean, it's not like I can write a book on my phone. I've got to get out my computer and start typing the keys."

"You write stories for the kids all the time on your phone. I hear you talking to your phone, telling your phone stories."

"I'm not telling it stories. It doesn't have a soul. It wouldn't like to hear my stories," he thought for a moment and then grew hopeful, "would it?"

"Maybe."

"I mean, no, I'm just dictating, and those are stories, not books. You can't write a story and call it a book. Especially not a fictionalized non-fiction self-help story narrative book."

"I thought you wanted to write a children's fantasy book?"

"Same thing."

"You've been going on and on about those tiny even atomic habits. You even recommend that all your readers read either Tiny Habits by BJ Fogg or Atomic Habits by James Clear available at all major book sellers. Can't you just use your phone as a tiny habit? It's easy to start. You can dictate some notes on your phone and then edit it on the computer later."

"It's not that easy."

"I thought you said it was easy."

"Well, yeah but not *that* easy. I have to make sure that the audiobook narrator makes sure to **emphasize** words that have ~~meaning~~ and that *takes* changes in **style** and ~~formatting~~. I mean, I just can't make writing a book any easier to start than browsing random articles on the internet or shopping for preowned stuff I don't want."

"Do you ever buy any preowned stuff on the internet?"

"I did once. It felt good to get a great deal."

"How much time did you spend looking for a great deal?"

"A lot more time than I would have spent working an extra hour to make ten times as much as I saved on that deal. Wow, when you put it that way."

"You put it that way."

"But it's still too easy. I mean, the link for the app is on my little menu bar at the bottom. The apps I use to write stories are buried in a folder somewhere."

"This seems like it is so simple I shouldn't even have to explain it to you or anyone else. Have you ever tried switching that around?"

"That's ridiculous. I can't switch that around. What if I need to access my browser quicker than my note-taking app? I might need to look something up like a random article. What if I need to buy something I really need right away? I need my pre-owned shopping app so that I can search for great deals on something they might possibly have at that time or some time in the future but if I save the, Oh." Forty-something dad stopped talking and then immediately started back up again.

"Just the time it took me to say all that, I could've been writing a book. I could've been sharing all that information that I've learned from reading books in a narrative format that might be more accessible to the average reader. Do you think there might be people out there who would rather read about how to improve their life in a more humorous and story format that might not otherwise read self-help books? This idea about a caveman having a conversation with a monkey comes to mind."

"Save that one for the kids but I think you're onto something. Maybe if you could make it more than slightly humorous."

Forty-something dad decided that for only once in his life he wouldn't listen to his wise wife. The monkey caveman thing sounded too good to let go of. Then the words of what she said after that sank in. He gasped a little too fast and choked on the air. "That's what I'll research next, how to make it funnier."

"Can I make a suggestion? You might consider giving that up a little bit more too. Researching and planning your next project before you even begin your first project might be just another form of procrastination."

"Hmm, I don't know about that. I think that's just planning ahead."

"How many plans have you made?"

"Thirty or forty, can't be too sure. I forget what I've already written about when I go off on a research tangent."

"That sounds a little like procrastination to me. By the way, have you noticed that the words I'm saying don't sound like the words I say? I'm a little more supportive than this. Are you putting words in my quotes?"

"Literary freedoms. I wouldn't worry about it."

"I think you should make your next chapter about focus. That's what seems to be the problem."

"Oh, I hear ya loud and clear, matey."

"And no pirates."

Focus

"Arr, me lens must be broken again," Pirate something dad said he lowered the spyglass.

"No, you've just got it turned the wrong way," said First mate. Pirate something dad never did like that First mate. He looked around for the other mates but remembered, sadly, that First mate was the only mate.

"No, it's not turned the wrong way. I've got it that way because I'm focusing on long-term goals. They're supposed to be far away. My lens is broken because I can't focus.

"The lens is supposed to go the other way so that it makes your long-term goals bigger. You can't focus unless you turn it the right way."

"Fine," pirate something dad smacked First mate on the head with the telescope and then turned it the other way. "It's not any better this way."

"Let me see that," First mate grabbed the spyglass and peered through the lenses. "There are no lenses in this spyglass."

"I know, I told you they were broken. That's why I took them out."

"You can't focus on anything through a spyglass without lenses. you might as well just curl your fingers around and put your hands together to make a pretend spyglass." First mate looked up to see pirate something dad curling his fingers around and putting his hands together to make a pretend spyglass.

"The spyglass is just a metaphor. I wouldn't be able to focus on my long-term term goals even if the lenses weren't broken. I am afraid I've come down with unfocusedivitus."

"That's not a thing."

"We are pirates. Anything is a thing."

"You're a pirate? You told me you were a merchant. You said this was a shipping vessel and you needed me to take inventory of the stock."

"That was a short-term goal. You didn't question the skull and crossbones flag?," he pointed up to the hand drawn flag that looked nothing like a skull or crossbones. "Anyway, that over there is our long-term goal," pirate something dad handed First mate the empty spyglass and pointed off into the distance.

He looked at the spyglass as it was handed to him but let it fall to the deck. He looked off where pirate something dad was pointing but didn't see anything. He squinted but still didn't see anything.

"I don't see anything."

"That's because you dropped the spyglass," pirate something dad explained.

"No, it's because there's nothing there."

Pirate something dad looked shocked and he quickly pulled up his two-handed pretend spyglass to look again.

"You're right. I've lost sight of my goals again. It's not there."

"What was it?"

"A book."

"What, are you going to read it?"

"No, write it."

"I see, and it was about pirates?"

"No, it's a children's fantasy adventure about," he mumbled the last word, "elves."

"Then why are we pirates?"

"Good question," Pirate something dad scratched his head.

"So, here's the problem. Your long-term goal is a book. The problem is, we are out here in the middle of the ocean."

"I see what you're saying. Books don't float. That's gonna be a problem. I've never written anything under the sea."

"That's not what I'm getting at. I think your problem is that you are out to sea," First mate put his hands on his hips and waited, hoping that pirate something dad would get what he was, not so subtly, hinting at.

"And you're afraid I can't swim. It's OK, I was a lifeguard when I was 16."

"That is one of those things that if you don't use it you lose it."

"Rats."

"Still not what I'm getting at."

"You think I shouldn't be a pirate? But the pirate was the good guy in monkey island and atlas shrugged."

"I think you should be focused on your goal. You gave up something so that you could achieve your goal but now you're doing something else."

"But I am still writing."

"This is just a metaphor."

"So you're saying that even though I give up something to start something else, if I still fill up all that time with other useless activities, I still won't achieve my goals?"

"Actually, you're saying that." First mate said.

"What do I do?"

"Focus. You gave up something so that you could do this thing that you have chosen to do. Why not do that instead of wasting your time doing something else?"

"How can I focus? I broke my lens."

"You don't need any special apps or extra discipline to focus on what you want. If you keep getting distracted like this, you either don't really want what you have set for a goal in the first place or you're too hesitant to try."

"I'm not scared!"

"I didn't say scared."

"But you meant scared."

"Are you scared?"

"Yes."

"Good," First mate said.

"Wait, what do I do about it?"

"That's an entirely different book."

"You're not going to tell me how to get over my fear?" Pirate something dad stepped forward on his peg leg making sure to thump every step.

"Just start with something super simple. Try an easy activity that will lead to the other activity. Do something you're not scared of now. If you want to write a fiction book, start with a little tiny fiction story."

"You mean, a pirate story."

"You could try that."

"So I'm not wasting time?" Pirate something dad asked.

"I wouldn't say that." First mate nodded politely and walked over to the edge of the ship. He jumped off and splashed through the three-inch deep water off toward the horizon.

"Hey, where are you going? There's going to be lots of sword fighting, pillaging and plundering stuff along the way," Pirate something dad called out. The First mate was already gone.

He looked off into the distance and saw the island he had been searching for in the first place. Pirate something dad turned the ship's wheel toward the island and waited. When nothing happened he sighed and jumped out of the boat to wade toward writers island. It was time to focus.

Give up Dreams

The middle-aged man sat up straight in bed in the middle of the night. Well, not the middle of the night but no one wakes up at this ungodly hour. He looked at the clock and shuddered, he overslept.

No time to brush teeth. That might lower his energy, maybe confidence? Either way, no time to brush teeth, he reminded himself as he brushed his teeth. At least he could skip tying the shoes that he never bothered to tie anyway.

The cold air slapped him in the face as he stepped out into the driveway. The garage door closed, no turning back now. Not unless he wanted to put the code in and open the garage door to go back inside. No, now he had to push through.

Forty-something dad thought about the distance he needed to run today. He wasn't going to be an Olympic runner if he didn't practice every day. He wasn't going to be an Olympic runner. That never had been a dream. It was all about a marathon. Then again, that was never a dream either. That was a nightmare. In fact, why was out here running at all? That wasn't even one of his goals. He hated running.

He did a couple of push-ups and went back inside. Yes, this was his goal, coffee and writing. Well, revisions, the writing part would come at some other random time whenever inspiration would hit him. If only inspiration would hit him.

He sat down at the desk and picked up his guitar. He would never be a world-class rock star if he didn't practice every day. He played two songs that he already knew. At least, he played part of the chorus and messed up most of the solo. He felt pretty good about it and set it back down. That might not entirely get him where he needed to be.

A little stretchy band on his desktop called him and told him it was a workout. He was never going to be a world-class bodybuilder if he didn't work out every day. He pulled on the band a couple of times and set it back down. That was a good workout even if the bodybuilders said stretchy band wouldn't cut it. Forty-something dad had a doctorate degree n something, he knew better than them even if it hadn't been working for the past several years.

Now, for the real reason he was here. What was the reason he was here? Coffee and writing, that was it. Only then did it occur to him, He hadn't practiced juggling today. He was not going to be a world-class juggler if he didn't practice every day.

The second hand on the clock kept moving further and further around the circle. The minute hand was following dangerously close. Time was getting away even at this ungodly hour of 6:37 AM. Crap, he had gotten up at 5:31 AM.

Forty-something dad still had several other dreams he had to work towards this morning. He needed to read. He was never going to be a world-class reader if he didn't practice every day. He needed to play some video games. He would never be a world-class, never mind. Even if that is a thing, that's not really a thing.

"Hey, you know, I kind of feel like all these other dreams are getting in the way of my dreams."

Forty-something dad, are you saying that you want to give up on some of your dreams?

"Well, I'm not a quitter but, giving up is essentially the theme of this book. Maybe I do need to give up on some of the dreams that I don't really want anymore."

He thought about that quite hard for a moment. Then with a heavy heart, he picked up his guitar and dropped it in the trashcan. The books, juggling balls, and stretchy band followed next. He pulled the juggling balls back out and started juggling again. Then he tossed them in the trash can.

Forty-something dad sat back down at his desk. The fancy zebrawood pin found its way into his hand on top of the blank piece of paper. A single tear escaped from the corner of his left eye. It raced down the contours between his nose and cheek until it jumped off to destroy his writing. Forty-something dad slammed down his pen and interrupted me.

"I don't cry. You can't put that in there. I just don't wanna give up all those other things. Maybe I don't have to."

He ran over to the trash can and pulled the guitar, books, and resistance bands out of the trashcan. The juggling balls, strangely, were already in his pocket.

"I don't have to give up on my hobbies. These are just for fun. I need fun. I need distractions. As long as I don't get distracted by them. I just need to give up the dreams that are either unrealistic or are not really my dream anymore, or ever were.

I don't have to be a rock star. I can just enjoy jamming with my son. I don't have to be a bodybuilder but maybe I can keep stretching this band just for fun. No, that's not fun. I will do it for the health benefits and to stay in shape. I don't have to be a world-class juggler," he stopped juggling for a moment and started again, "but maybe I will."

Forty-something dad, I feel you've made some real progress here today. You've learned that not all your dreams are worthy of your attention. Sometimes you need to give up just so that you can gain the time to work on what is your dream.

"I've really got to stop talking to myself out loud."

Time

Fortysomething dad lifted the corner of the rug. That's usually where everything was. Anytime he lost something, it always ended up underneath the rug. He blamed the dog. He looked up at me and shook his head, somehow blaming me.

He was right. It wasn't under the rug. It was never under the rug, it was always under the piano. He got down on his hands and knees, then dropped down on his belly. He smashed his cheek against the floor yet somehow, still, he could almost but not quite see under the piano. Oh well, it must not be under the piano. He wondered about all the stuff that might be under the piano that he had given up and said, "oh well, it must not be under the piano."

He already looked at the desk drawer twelve times but I knew there was a good possibility it could still be in the desk drawer. He opened it, rummaged around a little bit, and closed it again. What was he looking for? He hated the possibility but knew with certainty that it was probably in Eight-something son's room. He took a deep breath and stepped into the battlefield.

While some catchy music played in the background he found it quite odd that there was only a single straight path through the room. Obstacles lie in front of him and he couldn't really see off to either side. Nevertheless, he entered the room. A large green pipe stood in front of him. He couldn't quite climb up it but found that if he jumped straight up, he could easily land on top of it or fall on the other side.

A strange suspicion told him that he could find quite a few loose coins if he were to climb down inside of the green pipe. That will have to wait for another day. He was on a mission. He would soon remember what it was he was looking for, and coins certainly were not it.

As he jumped down he saw a mushroom coming toward him. Fortysomething dad screamed and jumped back up on the pipe. This all sounded a little too familiar and much too old for Eight-something son.

Something jumped on his head and then jumped off. He landed next to a mushroom and then jumped on top of it, squishing it to oblivion.

"What are you doing, Forty-something dad?"

"I'm looking for more time," he said. He'd lost time somewhere and was trying to find more of it. He was starting to think that he was not going to find it here in this bedroom video game.

He noticed his son was wearing pink. Not an odd color for a boy. Back in the 1920s, men wore pink as a power color. That was in hundred years ago. He watched as my son sucked some of his toys into his mouth then swallowed and became partially like those toys. That wasn't the right video game.

"I'm starting to think that this is not the best way to find time," Forty-something dad said.

"Of course not. This is the best way to spend time."

He had to agree with Kirby. This was not a place to find more time. Forty-something dad had to find something a little less entertaining to him personally that he could find time in.

He decided to go ahead and climb down the green tube. Unfortunately, there were no coins. Instead, he found an underlined string of blue text. It was strange. Together the letters and numbers and symbols made no sense. Separate, the letters, numbers, and symbols still made no sense.

He sniffed the blue words. He stared at the blue words but nothing happened. Finally, when He pushed them with his index finger, while his other fingers were curled down and his thumb still out, the whole world vanished. He found himself stranded out in a desert full of underlined blue strings of text. This would definitely be a place to find a lot of time lost in here.

He jumped from one blue text to another. Then back and to yet another. There had to be more time here. In one place he learned about multitasking every minute that he had available to take care of all the little things. Another place he learned about meditating, making sure he was not multitasking.

On yet another string of blue words, he found someone telling him he only needed twenty minutes of sleep every four hours. But then when he jumped to another one he found someone telling him if he didn't sleep eight hours a night he would die before seventy.

The more he searched for time, the more he found the secret to finding more time was not to be found on the little blue strings of text and symbols with another line.

"What are you looking for?" Five something daughter asked.

"Time," I just don't seem to have enough of it."

"I've got time. Do you wanna play chess?" She asked. As all Forty-something dads know, five-something daughters do not play chess.

"I'm sorry, I just don't have time."

It hit me all at once like a cliche of bricks on my pinky toe. This is what I've been looking for. Not a five-year-old who could play chess, though it is rare. He found the secret to finding time. He wanted this more than he wanted that.

He no longer need to find someone who had found a way to save or find more time. He didn't need 25-hour days. He didn't need someone to tell me what to give up to gain more time. All he needed was priorities.

"What is it you really want to prioritize?" Thirty-something daughter asked.

"What? No! This is not supposed to be a nightmare. Where did my Five-something daughter go? I wanted to spend time with her. I wanted to play chess, even though that's not what five-year-olds do. You have to give me back time."

"You can't get any of your time back. You have to choose right now what you want to spend your time doing. Would you rather research on the internet how to save time and get more done? Would you rather write a book or would you rather play chess with your five-year-old daughter and get nothing done?"

Eight-something son floated through the room and sucked up a little sword-fighting man. He swallowed him and became a sword-fighting pink blob.

"Or would you rather swallow bad guys with your son? It's not a complex problem even though most everyone seems to treat it as such. We have too many things now that occupy our time and not enough people willing to give up on the time wasters. You don't need to organize your candy so it can be crushed just to fill the time. Use that time for something you would rather do. Whenever you do something, ask yourself if that is what you want to be doing. If not, stop it and go do what you really want to do."

Forty-something dad didn't notice when he started playing the sad violin but he was almost in tears now. "It's not fair. He's still only eight years old. I can't believe I wasted the time. I didn't play chess with you when you were five. I didn't write a book. I never wrote the book for you that I wanted to because I was too busy searching for time. It's all been wasted time. Time is not on my side."

"Forty-something dad, I'm still five. I just sound like I'm thirty. I've been talking in full sentences since I was one."

"Oh, true, is that why you still look like you're five? Do you play chess like you're five or thirty?"

"That depends."

"Depends on what?"

"Whether or not I got a nap in kindergarten today and the answer is, yes I did."

"Either way, I consider this a good use of time."

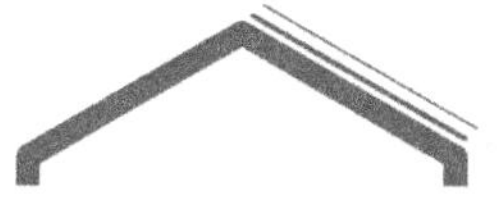

Does Everything Himself

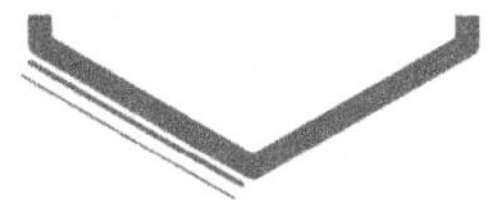

Forty-something picked up a nail and started to drive it into the wood. It bent so he pulled it out and tried another one. He flipped the hammer around and contemplated using the end with the big circle on it. That didn't make any sense so he flipped back around and banged with the curved side again. The electrician passed behind him with a big coil of wire. He threw it on the ground and let out a grunt.

"This works killing me," Electrician said.

"Aren't you an electrician? Isn't this what you do?" Forty-something dad asked. He turned to face the electrician and noticed he looked exactly like himself. So much so that this electrician was probably just another version of himself.

"No, I'm not an electrician. Not even sure why I'm doing this. Probably should've hired an electrician to do the electrical work."

"If you're not an electrician, why are you doing it?"

"No idea," not electrician said.

They both heard a loud explosion and turned to see the plumber come running out of the unfinished bathroom screaming and soaking wet.

"Don't go in there for at least 10 minutes," The plumber stopped to catch his breath.

"Why not?" Not electrician asked.

"That'll give me time to get away."

"What happened in there?" Forty-something dad asked.

"I don't know, I'm not a plumber." The not plumber said. He also looked like a soaking wet version of Forty-something dad. As the carpenter version of himself watched the others, he didn't watch where he was nailing and swung the hammer straight through the open wall frame. Someone on the other side shouted a few unpleasant words that fortysomething dads don't say if they might read a book to their kids.

"What are you doing," the not bricklayer burst through the open wall frame.

"I don't know, I'm not a carpenter," Forty-something dad said as he held out a hand for his hammer to be returned. The not brick layer shook his head and crossed his arms.

"Look, guys, if you're not construction workers, then why are you trying to build a house?" The actual roofer jumped down from the rafters. Everyone started shrugging and looking around pointlessly. Forty-something dad shrugged as well but then looked sheepishly down at his feet.

"If you want something done right, you've got to do it yourself?" he suggested.

"Well that's dumb," the maybe real roofer said. Oddly enough, he looked exactly like every single one of the other versions of Forty-something bad except with a shirt that said 'the roof is on fire.' He must be a roofer and he must be fortysomething.

"Hey, how does that work?" The not carpenter asked. "How are you a real roofer? I'm not a roofer. Am I you? Are you me?"

"No, you definitely are not. But you've got to start somewhere. You did put a couple of roofs on with friends back in college. Besides, *roofer* is the closest sounding to *writer* as you were going to get in this metaphor."

"I did do that. You know what, I really did not enjoy that."

"Well, then you better pick some other profession in this house-building metaphor that you can stick with and dig into. Do you wanna write a book? You don't need to be designing the cover, editing the book, marketing the book, and everything else in between. Pick the one thing and knock it out of the park."

"But I don't wanna pay anybody else to do all of this stuff. I don't plan on making any money off of the book so I can't really justify paying a carpenter, electrician, or plumber to do it all for me."

"Yeah but you're not a carpenter, plumber, electrician, or roofer. Do you want to be a writer? Stick with writing. Do you wanna be a roofer? Stick with roofing

"I thought I established that I don't want to be a roofer."

"That's what I'm saying. I hate to break it to you but you're wasting time again. You gave up something so that you could focus on one thing. Now you're focusing on ten things that you don't even really want to focus on. There's not much more benefit for you doing all this extra than what you were doing before."

"I used to spend my time playing games and browsing the preowned shopping apps on the internet."

"I see, and you couldn't think of something even a little less degrading to use as a metaphor?"

"Snapchat? Twitter? Whatapp? the one where people dance stupid?"

"Better, but you don't even know what those are so I doubt you wasted time with that."

"You're right. I've got to focus or else giving up something was worthless. Even though I don't really wanna go back to wasting my time doing literally nothing."

Forty-something dad decided to focus. He stared straight ahead and the roofer version of himself started to fade, *Back to the Future* style.

"No, not me. Get rid of these other guys first. I'm the one giving you advice."

"Yeah, you're too bossy. Read some Dale Carnegie," Forty-something dad continued to focus and the roofer vanished completely. Then he turned to the other not construction workers and started assigning jobs.

"You, plumber, you are now in charge of researching writing style. I want you to find out all the things that I should not do when I write. Better yet, find out what I should do in writing.

Not electrician, you're in charge of editing. I know, I'm not supposed to edit my own books but I can't send a rough draft, that I dictated to an editor. They won't even know what I'm trying to say. Siri doesn't usually know what I'm trying to say.

Everybody else, we're stopping all of our other projects. I know we got a lot of books planned to write but we got to focus on the one thing."

Everyone cheered but then one of the random workers raised his hand and asked, "what is the one thing we are going to focus on?"

"This house, it's about to fall down on top of us," Forty-something dad said as the roof collapsed and squished everyone.

Wasting Time Writing a Book (which is what he wanted to do in the first place).

Forty-something dad pulled the chair out at his desk and stepped around to sit down. As his butt came closer to the chair, the seat slid out on its own. He landed on the floor a little more confused than embarrassed. After all, no one was watching.

Five-something daughter and Eight-something son started laughing. Forty-something dad stood back up and wrestled the chair into submission. He planted his butt firmly in the seat, which started bucking like a bronco.

He rode the wild ride, gripped with fear. The kids started cheering from the other side of the room. Then, Forty-something dad started to enjoy it. He held on with one hand and raised his other hand up like a rodeo cowboy.

"You show that chair who's boss," Eight-something son shouted.

"Yeah, you ride that chair, Forty-something dad."

While he wanted to correct her and force his daughter to continue calling him 'daddy,' he felt quite encouraged that she was cheering him on. Give it another five years and it will come out more as an embarrassed and extended 'daaaaad.'

Finally, the chair broke. Not in a literal sense but more like a wild horse. It settled down into a nice steady rhythm. Forty-something dad picked up the pen to do what he had come here to do. As he put the pen to paper, it jumped back up to his face.

Grabbing the pen with both hands, Forty-something dad forced it back down to the blank page. It pulled to the left. When he pulled to the right, the pen switched and forced itself over to the left.

The pen jumped up out of his hands and began writing all over Forty-something dad's face. It was gibberish, it was nonsense. It was the kind of stuff that Forty-something dad wrote anyway. The only problem was that it was on his face.

"Yay!" both kids cheered from the other side of the room.

"You're supposed to be cheering for me. The pen is winning."

The kids both looked at each other and shrugged. They looked back at Forty-something dad and started clapping when the pen started writing on his face again.

"Can we go play now?" Five-something daughter asked.

"No, you're supposed to be supporting me," he had a hold of the pen with both hands pulling it back from his face.

"We can support you better from the other room," Eight-something son said. That sounded like a good idea.

"OK, just cheer for me from the other room," he spoke to an empty room. The cheers from the next room had nothing to do with his fight against the pen and all to do with the battle between good and evil and stuffed puppies and monkeys. Fortunately, the pen was starting to behave.

It was in his hand. It was writing and not on his face. He wrote on the inside of his arm but it was closer to the page.

"Stop it, pen," he ordered.

The pen stuck its tongue out. Forty-something dad covered it up and tried like a parent, not to let it get to him. He closed his eyes and tried to ignore what was being written. It was written on the walls. It was written on the desk. It was written underneath the chair.

"What are you doing?" An angel appeared at the door.

"No, let's keep it realistic," Forty-something mom suggested. "You can just set me as a goddess or something." She set down a cup of coffee on the desk. The pen immediately revolted and started writing on the coffee cup.

"I'm trying to write," Forty-something dad answered her original question. "I know, I'm just wasting time again. Look at this mess."

"Looks like you're getting some ideas down."

"Yeah, but is it worth what I gave up?"

"What did you give up?"

"Um, Wasting time on those random articles about celebrities I don't know or like and randomly shopping for stuff I don't want to buy, usually on my phone?!,;" Forty-something dad wasn't quite sure what punctuation he should use there.

"Looks to me like you're getting some good ideas out. I would think they would be worth it."

"But there's nothing on the paper," he threw down the pen in disgust even though it somehow wrote discussed. It landed point down on the paper and stared indignantly back at him.

"I thought you dictated most everything anyway?"

Forty-something dad was hit with a sudden realization of great truth. He looked over at his other hand which had been pressing the microphone dictation on his phone the whole time. His jaw dropped and then he stuck his tongue out at the pin.

"You mean I did it?"

"I think you did it."

"I actually did something I wanted to do during the time that I gave up of what I would have been wasting time."

"Remember, time is limited. We've all only got the same amount of time. If you waste your time killing time, that you could have been pursuing your dreams, you are essentially killing dreams, by killing time."

"How come I never get to see the wise inspirational wisdom at the end of the story?" Forty-something dad questions.

"Aren't you writing this?"

"Sometimes I wonder," Forty-something dad looked down at the pen lying on its side. It stuck a tongue back out again.

"So does that mean that I will never get to waste time again?" Forty-something dad pulled out a few random balls and started juggling.

"I wouldn't say that. But if there's something that you would rather be doing, why not do that instead of wasting time avoiding doing something you want to do?

"Just so you know, juggling is not a waste of time and this is not a metaphor for anything. I really do like to juggle. It calms me and helps me use my whole brain."

And so Forty-something dad finished his book. He went on to write several more books but that is a story for another time because he hasn't done that yet. This is not one of the books that he finished in the story he wrote about, Forty-something dad will probably write more of these books as he learns more. He might even add chapters as he learns more and it becomes more relevant, like he did just now.

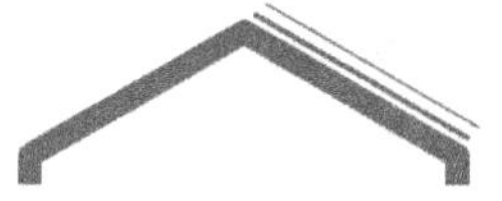

Gives Up Fear Of Failure

Forty-something dad leaned back in the reclining beach chair to speak to the psychoanalyst just like they did in the 1930s. It suddenly occurred to him that this was nothing at all like how they did it even in the 1930s.

"So, tell me what you're scared of," a high-pitched, squeaky, and not at all soothing voice came from behind. Psychoanalysts never liked the client to look them in the eye. Forty-something dad knew from modern psychology, that was probably the worst way to help someone with a problem but this analyst probably had something to hide.

"Well, I'm afraid of a lot of things. I'm afraid of dinosaurs, failure, black holes, oh yeah, and mice with lasers."

"I see, and of that list which do you think is the most realistic?"

"Mice with lasers is a close second. Black holes definitely don't exist. So I would have to say that failure is probably the biggest fear on that list."

"Well then, we've got to help you face your fear."

"What? I don't wanna face my fear. I wanna overcome it."

"No, sorry, you've got to face it to overcome it."

"I don't wanna argue with you because Dale Carnegie said never to argue but that's totally wrong. If I face my fear of failure, I'm going to fail, and then I'm just going to give up."

"I see, and how exactly would you go about it?"

"Well, I've got to start small. The big picture is what I'm scared of so if I start much smaller it won't be as scary. Then even if I do fail, I'll be willing to try again."

"Go on," the squeaky psych said.

"OK, so I break it down to the small steps and, wait a minute. Is this what you were trying to get me to say all along?"

"Possibly."

"Good work. OK, so if the problem is that I'm afraid to fail, and I break it down into something small enough that it doesn't sadden me if I do fail, then it won't be so hard to pick up the pieces of my broken heart and start again.

"Yes, but there's more, isn't there?"

"I don't think so, unless, wait a minute, you are good. The dinosaurs?"

"No."

"Mice with lasers?"

"That's just ridiculous," a sound not too unlike one of those Star Wars laser sword thingies came from the psychoanalyst. When Forty-something dad tried to turn and look, he snapped, "Focus, you've convinced yourself how to fail and accept it. Now how do you overcome that fear of failure?"

"Right," dad focused a little more. He tried to pull the reclining beach chair back up into a sitting position but someone had locked it into an awkward yet comfortable position. "Now that I am ok with failing at small things I can try to improve until I can succeed."

"No, you don't even need to succeed at the small things. You just need to try the small things. We are not even working on you succeeding right now. It's just overcoming your fear of failure."

"If I'm not afraid of the small things, I can try something a little bigger."

"Good, you do need some success though."

"If I keep trying and focusing on improving, eventually I will succeed some of the time."

"You'll need more successes than failures."

"I will need to focus my skills," Forty-something dad was getting excited. He tried to sit up and look at the psych but the reclining beach chair was just too comfortable. He leaned back and thought some more. "I need to focus my emotions."

"Not your emotions. Focus your cognition."

"That's not really a thing."

"Cognition is your interpretation of emotions."

"Scared is not an emotion."

"Scared is definitely an emotion. Fear is an emotion tied to an event or object."

"If I can trick my brain into thinking I am excited instead of scared when I think I'm going to fail, I might accidentally succeed."

"Doubt it."

"But maybe I won't be scared?"

"Maybe you'll be excited."

"I am excited."

"And what are you excited about."

"Failing!"

"Wrong."

"The possibility of failing?"

"Wronger."

"I am excited about doing something so challenging that I might fail but I know in the end if I give up my fear of failure, I will succeed gloriously."

"Yes, but with fewer adverbs and commas. What else are you excited about and not scared of anymore?"

"Mice with lasers."

Forty-something dad finally pulled himself out of the awkwardly comfortable reclining beach chair, stumbled to his feet, and turned. He jumped and screamed when he realized that his psychoanalyst was actually a giant mouse holding a Star Wars laser thingy.

"And are you scared?" Squeaky psych asked.

"No, I was thinking more of a Mickey Mouse with a laser beam attached to his forehead type of evil creepy. This giant field mouse with a Star Wars laser sword is pretty cool."

Gives Up Fear Of Success

When they told him it was a rope bridge across the ravine, Forty-something dad did not think that it was just a rope across the ravine. The word bridge implies more.

He started out walking across like a tight rope on the not tight rope. Dads don't have that kind of balance. Especially not if their kids stop going to tae-kwon-do.

"Hey, you can't blame this on me," Eight-something son shouted from the other side.

"Hey, you're on the wrong side. How did you get to the other side?"

"This is the side you started on."

"Did I already make it this far? Why did I turn around? I'm headed back in your direction," he slipped and fell, then hung by his hands.

"I think you're afraid,"

"I am not afraid," Forty-something dad's fingers trembled as he let go only slightly with one hand to inch forward or backward, he wasn't sure anymore, and only just a couple of centimeters. "You don't have to show that I'm afraid. I can tell you, that I'm not afraid. What could I possibly be afraid of? I listen to Tony Robbins, Mel Robbins, and Christopher Robin.

I even listen to the homeless guy on YouTube in the undershirt and long beard."

"Was that about overcoming fears?"

"No, he was trying to sell me tax liens."

"Why would you want to buy that?"

"I don't. He had a trashy t-shirt and an unkempt beard. Anyway, I'm not afraid to fail. If I fell right now, I would probably crash and burn but I'd get back up and cliche again."

"You mean, try, try again?"

"That is literally, exactly what I said."

"Yes but that's not the problem," Eight-something son snacked on something that his father really wanted right now but didn't know what it was. " You're not afraid to fail. You're afraid to succeed."

"That's not a thing."

"You need to be more confident that you will succeed so that I will be more confident that I can succeed." Eight-something son said as he finished his snack and started on tomorrow's snack.

"My fear of success has nothing to do with your fear of success," Forty-something dad said.

"So you admit it? You are afraid to succeed?"

"I didn't say that. I mean, I did say it but I didn't mean what I said. You tricked me. OK fine. What if I do succeed? What if everybody finds out that I am a failure who succeeded?"

"If a failure succeeds, doesn't that make him a success?"

"Yeah but it's not supposed to be. Failures don't succeed. Successors succeed," Dad reminded.

"You've got to reprogram your brain. You've got to be ready for success. You've got to give up your fear of success."

"I was wondering how that fit in here. Another thing that I have to give up."

"It's wasting your time. All that second-guessing. You are wasting more energy worrying about how everyone will see you if you do succeed in what you're trying to do."

"OK, how do I reprogram my brain?"

"I am an eight-year-old boy. Do you really think I have an answer to that?"

"Yes."

"Good because I do! OK, we got to plug your brain into my Chromebook from school. First I need to drill some holes in your head."

"I have a better idea. Why don't we both just keep focusing on our successes? I've succeeded at other things before, right? I mean I woke up this morning. That's a success already. Oh, yeah and the whole graduate school thing and successful career blah blah blah. I'm feeling better about this already. Lets both you and me, focus on our successes. instead of thinking about how we failed at anything, let's ask ourselves what we will do next time and what we are going to do this time to make it right."

"Hey, that's a good idea."

"Really, you think so?"

"What? Oh, don't mind me, I was watching an advertisement. They suggested that I talk my dad into buying me some of these new plastic toys or snacks."

"Plastic snacks? OK, focus on success. Forty-something dad reached out to scratch his beard.

"Oh, and don't touch your face."

"Yeah, I know, it's a sign of insecurity body language but I can't put my hands in my pockets either."

"No, I meant if you're touching your face that means you're not holding onto the rope."

"I see, that does kind of ruin my metaphor of hanging at the end of my rope."

"I never did get that one," Eight-something boy had another snack just to break up the conversation and add more background detail. This one smelled like crackers which have no smell.

"Well, how can I succeed now? I've fallen into the bottom of the ravine," Forty-something dad was standing on the floor a few inches below arms reach of the rope bridge rope.

"Why don't you use the ladder, the stairs, or the elevator?"

"Is it really that easy?" Forty-something dad asked.

"The last step usually is. You've put in all the hard work already. All you gotta take is that last step. Let's say you wrote a book, hypothetically, since that's what this is really all about. You put in all the revisions you had the cover art created and you've even done quite a bit of marketing. All you gotta do is click the publish button."

"It's that easy? I mean, if I had already put in that work, hypothetically. If I was writing a book about something."

"Did you already write a book?"

"Yes, but not this one. This is a book on how to give up something so that you can find the time to write the other book or learn guitar or stand-up comedy."

"I thought you said that only quitters give up?"

"Never give up! Except, give up everything I told you to give up in this story," Forty-something dad climbed the stairs with his feet, the ladder with his hands, and pushed the button on the elevator with his nose, to publish.

Don't miss out!

Visit the website below and you can sign up to receive emails whenever J Edward Frank publishes a new book. There's no charge and no obligation.

https://books2read.com/r/B-A-JPXR-OXVZB

BOOKS 2 READ

Connecting independent readers to independent writers.

Also by J Edward Frank

Fortysomething Dad Self Help Stories
Give up to Gain

Watch for more at https://jedwardfrank.wordpress.com.

About the Author

J Edward is probably reading right now. Either that or writing stories even when he is supposed to be doing someting else. He figured out early that the best way to learn anything is to make a story. He went to college and got some degrees...and then more degrees, but it wasn't until he started reading on his own, about personal development that he started to wonder if he might be able to make a ridiculous story to help him remember everything. After that worked marvelously, he want everyone else to see what humor could do for learning. Now he has devoted his life, or at least some of his spare time, to helping everyone learn the concepts to live a full life, without having to read big long books.

Read more at https://jedwardfrank.wordpress.com.

About the Publisher

Highway One Publishing strives to bring the best books to the people who want to read them most.